THE LITTLE BOOK OF
BARCELONA

Published in 2022 by OH!
An Imprint of Welbeck Non-Fiction Limited,
part of Welbeck Publishing Group.
Based in London and Sydney.
www.welbeckpublishing.com

ISBN 978-1-80069-187-2

Compiled and written by Catherine Stephenson
Project manager: Russell Porter
Design: Tony Seddon
Production: Jess Brisley

A CIP catalogue record for this book is available from the British Library

Printed in China

10 9 8 7 6 5 4 3 2 1

Illustrations: shutterstock.com

THE LITTLE BOOK OF

BARCELONA

THE MEDITERRANEAN CAPITAL
OF CULTURE AND COOL

CONTENTS

INTRODUCTION

There's no other city quite like Barcelona. To start with is its unique setting on the Mediterranean, confined by one river to the north and another to the south, the rocky outcrop of Montjuïc, and the Collserola mountain range topped by Tibidabo.

City residents are spoiled with equal access to both the mountains and sea, in what is one of the most avant-garde and cosmopolitan cities in Europe. Plus, Barcelona isn't just any big city – it's the capital of Catalonia, one of Spain's richest and most highly industrialized regions, proud of its own identity and language, and independent-minded.

Barcelona is a very compact city, which, with its efficient bus and metro networks, makes getting about a piece of cake. Locals complain of rents having soared over the past 10 years, and undoubtedly the city's popularity as a tourist destination is at least partly responsible. Barcelona is used to welcoming 12 million visitors a year.

But then, who doesn't want to visit Barcelona? Back in 1862, Hans Christian Andersen described it as the "Paris of Spain". Today, its rich history and culture is indisputable. The jewels in its crown are, arguably, the Catalan Art Nouveau buildings gifted by Gaudí and his contemporaries. However, the city is blessed with a host of famous landmarks. The three most famous – the Sagrada Família, the Picasso Museum and Camp Nou – most succinctly represent the city's greatest religions of design, art and football.

Modern Barcelona has 10 idiosyncratic districts and an impressive 73 neighbourhoods, each with its own distinctive flavour. It packs in a dizzying number of bars and restaurants. The all too reasonably priced drinks, a sunny terrace on every corner, Mediterranean-centred cuisine and a nightlife that doesn't get going until well after the sun goes down make the city a place that's easy to be in – and difficult to leave.

CHAPTER
ONE

Barcelona Unfolded

Today's Barcelona was forged by a string of different civilizations and cultures over a period of more than 2,000 years. No wonder its spirited people are proud! It was founded by the Romans as a strategic post at the mouth of the Llobregat River.

How times have changed for the small settlement they named Barcino, now an undisputed metropolis in its own right.

It was on a summer's day in Barcelona, in July 1936, that the opening shots were fired in what was to become the Spanish Civil War.

The city finally fell to General Franco's forces on 26 January 1939.

"

It appeared that even in Barcelona there were hardly any bullfights nowadays; for some reason all the best matadors were Fascists.

"

George Orwell, *Homage to Catalonia*, 1938

During Franco's dictatorship (1939–75), not only were democratic freedoms suppressed, but also the Catalan language, which was excluded from the education system and relegated to the family sphere.

Castilian (Spanish) became the only language of education, administration and the media.

The faded but beautiful little square of Sant Felip Neri in the Gothic Quarter has lived through dark moments. A plaque and the shrapnel scars on the church façade remind us of the fact that a bombing raid by Franco's planes ended the lives of 42 people, many of them children who had sought refuge in the air-raid shelter. Today, children skip around the fountain, unaware of the tragic history.

Hotel Continental, at 138 La Rambla, is where George Orwell and his wife, Eileen, stayed in 1937 in the middle of the civil war.

Orwell was recruited into the International Brigade and fought alongside the Republicans on the front lines in Aragon.

His experience is described in the book *Homage to Catalonia.*

66

About midday on 3 May a friend crossing the lounge of the hotel said casually: 'There's been some kind of trouble at the Telephone Exchange, I hear.' … I was half-way down the Ramblas when I heard several rifle-shots behind me. I turned round and saw some youths, with rifles in their hands and the red and black handkerchiefs of the Anarchists round their throats…

99

George Orwell, *Homage to Catalonia*, 1938

> 66
>
> The haunting of history is
> ever present in Barcelona. I see
> cities as organisms, as living
> creatures. To me, Madrid
> is a man and Barcelona is a
> woman. And it's a woman
> who's extremely vain.
>
> 99

Carlos Ruiz Zafón

Refugi 307, at 109 Nou de la Rambla, is where the residents of Poble Sec took refuge from the bombings of the civil war.

It consists of 400 m (1,300 ft) of tunnel measuring 1.6 m (5.2 ft) wide and 2 m (6.5 ft) high, with toilets, fountains and an infirmary, and can now be visited as part of the Museu d'Història de la Ciutat (City History Museum).

From the 1920s to the 1960s,
tides of immigrants came
to work in Barcelona from
impoverished areas of Spain,
but often found no other place
to live than the shanty towns
that spread along the coastline
and up the hills.

Most of the slums had no
running water, light or
sanitation.

66

Barcelona was a most
illustrious city for its princes
and most noble – its knights;
its richness and great
prosperities were known
all over the world for being
marvellous and vigorous, and
therefore, exposed to envy.

99

Lucio Marineo Siculo

Irish author Colm Tóibín described the Barceloneta of the mid-1980s as an "overcrowded fishing village," noting that the water was so filthy that "nobody in his or her right mind would go down there for a swim."

This all changed when it was announced that Barcelona would host the 1992 Olympic Games. One of the key objectives was to open the city up to the sea, redeveloping the coastline from Barceloneta to what is now the Fòrum.

Barcelona was founded by
the Romans who set up a colony
called Barcino at the end of the
1st century BC. It prospered, grew
and was walled during the
4th century.

As a result, when the Roman
Empire fell apart, the Visigothic
king Ataulf turned it into the capital
of his kingdom, which extended
through Spain and France.

The underground ruins of
the Roman city of Barcino
were stumbled upon by chance
in 1930.

Today, you can visit the Museu
d'Història de la Ciutat and see
the ruined frescoes, old city
walls, and even giant basins for
wine storage.

"

Marseilles, Barcelona, Trieste,
Istanbul – each romances
the Mediterranean in its own
fashion, mostly by embracing
the sea in sweeping C-shaped
bays that date back to antiquity.

"

André Aciman

One of the city's golden eras was in Middle Ages, when the different Catalan territories came together under the countship of Barcelona and under the shadow of the Frankish kings.

This union was the foundation for the Catalan expansion in the Mediterranean in the 13th to 15th centuries.

During the Middle Ages,
Barcelona became a destination
for merchants, artisans and sailors,
who gathered in centrally located
guilds in the La Ribera and
El Born districts.

Some of the narrow streets in these
areas today bear the names of
medieval trades and guilds, such
as the streets of "Flassaders" and
"Sombrerers" (bedspread makers
and hat makers respectively).

"

It is a little and beautiful
city, situated near the
seashore … Traders with
merchandises come to it from
all over: from Greece, Pisa,
Alexandria, the Holy Land,
Africa and all its surroundings.

"

Benjamin of Tudela, 12th century

Barcelona features strongly in the history of the famous novel *Don Quixote,* as well as being the setting for some chapters in the book's second part.

Barcelona's Cervantes Street is named after the author, Miguel de Cervantes, and is where the first complete edition of *Don Quixote* was printed in 1617.

66

Barcelona, archives of
courtesy, shelter of the
foreigners, hospital of the
poor, fatherland of the brave,
vengeance of the offended and
pleasant correspondence of
firm friendship, and in site,
and in beauty, unique.

99

**Don Quixote recollects Barcelona in the second
part of *Don Quixote* by Miguel de Cervantes, 1615**

Opposite the Santa Maria
del Mar church, at El Fossar
de les Moreres (Mulberry
Cemetery), a flame burns
brightly over a steel arch,
in memory of the Catalan
resistance fighters who were
buried here after the Siege of
Barcelona ended in defeat,
in September 1714.

La Boqueria is one of the oldest
markets in the world.

While the current structure was erected in
1840, at the beginning of the 13th century
there was an open-air street market in the
same location on La Rambla, which was
just outside the city gates.

Farmers and traders from the surrounding
villages would gather here to sell their
produce and save on the tax for bringing
goods into the city.

One summer's day in 1859, a strange-looking wooden vessel slid into the Barcelona port. It chugged about for a few minutes and then sank as onlookers watched in grave silence. Twenty minutes later, the vessel emerged from the muddy green water.

This was *Ictineo*, the first steam-powered submarine. It was designed by Narcís Monturiol i Estarriol, a self-taught engineer.

The triangular patch of land extending into the sea that houses the charming Barceloneta district did not exist until the 15th century. It was then that the island of Maians, little more than a reef, was absorbed by the city in the construction of Barcelona's first port.

Over the subsequent centuries, the peninsula was enlarged and a fisherman's shanty town sprang up.

The notoriously tiny apartments in the Barceloneta fishing district are referred to as *quarts de casa* ("quarter houses").

FC Barcelona supporters celebrate their victories at the Canaletes fountain on La Rambla.

This tradition dates back to the days when the sports newspaper *La Rambla* had its offices in front of the fountain.

Fans congregated there on Sundays to find out match results, which were posted via a blackboard in the window.

Not many hospitals can boast stained-glass windows, paintings and mosaics in buildings surrounded by faultless landscaping and ornate statues of gargoyles and angels.

Hospital de la Santa Creu i Sant Pau is the largest Art Nouveau complex in the world, built by Catalan architect Lluís Domènech i Montaner in 1930, and was a fully functioning hospital until 2009.

Today this UNESCO World Heritage Site is open to visitors.

Els Quatre Gats tavern was the retreat for Avant Garde artists and writers to exchange ideas. It was frequented by the young Picasso, who put on his first show here in 1900.

You may have seen it in Woody Allen's film *Vicky Cristina Barcelona*.

The creator of Els Quatre Gats, Pere Romeu, drew his inspiration for the tavern's décor from the famous French café called Le Chat Noir ("The Black Cat").

However, he gave it a Catalan name, Els Quatre Gats ("The Four Cats"), an expression that means "only a few people" and which can be used to describe those who are seen as a bit odd or as outsiders.

Like most of Gaudí's masterpieces, Casa Milà
has no straight lines or right angles.

The whole façade is made from large stone
slabs that were attached to the structure,
for stonemasons to work on them. Initially
ridiculed by the local community, the building's
rocky appearance and strange undulating shape
lent it its nickname "The Quarry".

"

Curved lines
belong to God.

"

Antoni Gaudí

CHAPTER
TWO

So Much More than Gaudí

Barcelona has ancient architectural treasures – the temple columns, city walls and underground stone passages left by the Romans – but equally, if you stroll through the Gothic Quarter, you will find yourself transported to medieval Barcelona, with its quaint churches and quiet squares.

And perhaps most famously, moving into the Eixample district and beyond, are the masterpieces of *modernisme* or Catalan Art Nouveau.

Barcelona's 10 administrative districts

Ciutat Vella
Eixample
Sants-Montjuïc
Les Corts
Sarrià-Sant Gervasi
Gràcia
Horta-Guinardó
Nou Barris
Sant Andreu
Sant Martí

The beautiful church of
Santa Maria del Mar was built in
the 14th century in the La Ribera
district, when this was the seafront.

The story of its construction is
told in the novel *The Cathedral of
the Sea* by Ildefonso Falcones.

Designed by Berenguer de
Montagut, it is held to be a
paradigm of the best Catalan
Gothic architecture.

Home to the city's nobles in medieval times, Montcada Street is lined with a succession of beautiful medieval, Renaissance and Baroque mansions, with majestic doorways, suitable for horses and carriages, and each with a spacious central courtyard inside that leads to the first floor via a beautiful staircase.

Today, many of these former homes house museums, such as the Museu Picasso.

"

Here in Barcelona, it's the architects who built the buildings that made the city iconic who are the objects of admiration – not a bunch of half-witted monarchs.

"

Julie Burchill

66

The essence of the great Barcelona,
the eternal, the incorruptible, the grand,
is on this street, which has a Gothic
side where you can hear clear Roman
fountains and the afternoon prayer, and
another motley, cruel, incredible side,
where you can hear the accordions of
all the sailors in the world and there is a
night flight of painted lips and peals of
laughter at dawn.

99

Federico García Lorca

In the Gothic Quarter, you will come across a number of stone sculptures of women's heads from the 17th century, called Les Carasses. They were used to mark the location of brothels.

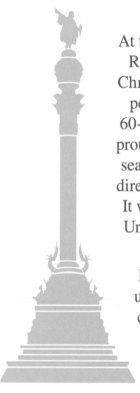

At the lower end of La Rambla, a statue of Christopher Columbus perches on top of a 60-m (197-ft) column, proudly pointing out to sea (though not in the direction of America!). It was erected for the Universal Exhibition of 1888.

If you take a lift up to the top, you can enjoy a 360º bird's-eye view of the city.

Architect Antoni Gaudí's
work reflects his fascination
with the natural world.

Shunning straight lines,
he favoured the use of organic
curves that mirror the way
objects such as trees, shells,
plants and rocks are formed.

Gaudí's awe-inspiring Sagrada Família church is today the undisputed icon of Barcelona.

Its construction began in 1882, but was halted in 1926 when the architect was tragically run over by a tram. Construction resumed and a succession of architects have since sought to decipher Gaudí's complex designs.

It is hoped that the building will be completed by 2026.

66

There are no
straight lines or sharp
corners in nature.
Therefore, buildings must
have no straight lines or
sharp corners.

99

Antoni Gaudí

66

I went to have a look at
the cathedral – a modern
cathedral, and one of the
most hideous buildings
in the world.

99

George Orwell on the Sagrada Família

The department store El Corte Inglés ("The English Cut") is a Spanish institution.

The store on Plaça de Catalunya provides a fabulous view over Barcelona from its top-floor cafeteria.

Natural light pours through the stained-glass windows and inverted glass dome of the Catalan Art Nouveau's Palau de la Música Catalana.

This makes it the only concert hall in the world that is illuminated entirely by natural light during daylight hours.

"

At Barcelona, we had the pleasure of seeing the Fandango danced. It exceeds in wantonness all the dances I ever beheld. A good Fandango lady will stand five minutes in one spot, wriggling like a worm that has just been cut in two.

"

Henry Swinburne

Known as the "Hotel
Vela" (Sail Hotel) owing
to its distinctive shape,
the five-star hotel
W Barcelona, designed
by Ricardo Bofill, stands
on land reclaimed from
the sea.

The emblematic El Molino ("The Windmill") music hall was founded in 1898 and a small stage was set up for flamenco concerts.

At that time, the mythical Parallel Avenue hummed with theatres, music halls, cabarets and cafés, and was known as the Barcelona Montmartre.

Camp Nou,
FC Barcelona club's
home stadium is
the biggest in Europe,
and the fourth largest
association football
stadium in the world.

Camp Nou in numbers

55,000 square metres
(592 square feet)

99,354 seats

52 sprinklers

107 doors

50 emergency exits

As part of an ambitious City Council plan to reduce pollution and noise levels, Barcelona's first *superilles* (superblocks) were created in 2016. These mini car-free neighbourhoods, each consisting of nine blocks, restrict traffic to major roads outside.

The plan is that more than 500 will eventually be built, starting in the famous gridded neighbourhood of Eixample.

After almost a decade of work and an investment of 80 million euros, the vast Mercat de Sant Antoni, originally designed by architect Antoni Rovira i Trias between 1879 and 1882, reopened its doors in 2019.

This giant market spreads over five floors, four of which are underground.

"

The most joyful street in the world, the street where all the four seasons live together. The only street I wish would never end. Rich in sounds, abundant in breeze, beautiful in its encounters, old in its blood: Rambla de Barcelona.

"

Federico García Lorca

The five streets making up Las Ramblas*

Rambla de Canaletes

Rambla dels Estudis

Rambla de Sant Josep
(or de les Flors)

Rambla dels Caputxins

Rambla de Santa Mònica

* "Les Rambles" in Catalan

66

Down the Ramblas, what a dream!
In no other country will you see flower
stalls so full and bursting with life.
In a bucket, a dazzling bunch of red
carnations! Roses with silk petals.
Over there, some violets, white broom
flowering: full branches of it, and roses,
roses and more roses! Sant Jordi
is coming.

99

**Mercè Rodoreda, Catalan storyteller
and novelist (1908–83)**

"

The stands on the Rambla were bursting with white and red roses … Between the stands of red roses, a grey man of indeterminate cheeks and age wobbled a bit as he walked, his stomach full of whisky and his heart full of red roses.

"

Josep Maria de Sagarra, Catalan poet, playwright and author (1894–1961)

❝

After a while dawn tinged the sky with amber, and Barcelona woke up. We heard the distant bells from the basilica of Santa Maria del Mar, just emerging from the mist on the other side of the harbour.

❞

Carlos Ruiz Zafón,
The Shadow of the Wind, 2001

The Les Glòries area boasts three new bold and modern landmark buildings: the Museu del Disseny de Barcelona (Design Museum), known as "The Stapler"; the soaring, shimmering Torre Glòries (formerly Agbar); and Mercat dels Encants, a flea market beneath a mirrored canopy.

Barcelona's Encants Vells is one of the oldest flea markets in Europe, dating back to the 14th century.

Today, it houses 500 stalls under a huge mirrored canopy.

The vast Fòrum esplanade
is the second-largest
public square in the world,
after Tiananmen Square.
It houses a huge
photovoltaic panel, the
size of a football field.

Barcelona Cathedral is renowned for its Gothic architectural style, with its pointed archways, the ribbed vaults visible from inside the building, and the gargoyles on the roof. However, the facade is actually a neo-Gothic 19th-century addition.

22@ is the name given to the urban renewal area in the former industrial area of Poblenou, dubbed "the Catalan Manchester" in the 19th century.

Begun during the 2000s and spanning 115 blocks, it is part of one of Europe's biggest urban regeneration schemes.

The latest addition to the iconic Barcelona skyline is the luminous Star of Bethlehem.

This colossal 12-point star, lit up for the first time on 8 December 2021, now adorns the tip of the Virgin Mary tower of La Sagrada Família.

The steel and glass structure weighs 5.5 tonnes, is 7.5 m (25 ft) wide and cost €1.5 million.

66

Barcelona the beautiful
and wise, where I left so
many things hanging on
the altar of happiness.

99

Pablo Picasso

CHAPTER
THREE

From Art to El Barça

Barcelona has produced many famous artists, who today have their own dedicated museums (Picasso, Miró or Tapies) – but this is only the tip of the iceberg. They sit alongside traditional Catalan customs and celebrations, not to mention the city's football, world-famous gastronomy and café culture.

FC Barcelona is member-owned, which makes it very rare among football clubs. It has over 144,000 members who make the decisions, and fans are encouraged to become members. The motto *Més que un club* ("More than a club") refers to the fact the club is democratic and owned by supporters.

"

The fans truly own this club. They decide its destiny and how it is managed.

"

Ferran Soriano, former vice president of FC Barcelona

FC Barcelona is the world's richest football club in terms of revenue, topping the Forbes list in 2021 with a valuation of $4.76 billion.

66

I think Barcelona and the Spanish national team have been good for soccer because there are a lot of teams that come up playing from the back: with the goalie, the defence, moving up a defender to midfield, playing attacking soccer. I think fans want to see that. They want to see beautiful soccer, a spectacle, and Barcelona does that.

99

Xavi, Manager of FC Barcelona

Barça supporters are called *culers*. The nickname dates back to when they used to watch the game at their old football ground at Indústria Street – they would often sit on a wall, from which their backsides (*culs*, in Catalan) protruded.

66

Barcelona is an open
and multicultural city. It's
brimming with a very special
creative energy. If you pay
attention, you may be easily
inspired by the places and
people living there.

99

Rosalía

"

Barcelona is one of my favourite cities in the world. The fashion and people are just so effortlessly cool.

"

Leigh Lezark

One of the most unique
Catalan traditions is the
"human towers". *Castellers*
build towers reaching heights
of more than 8 m (26 ft),
with children as young as
five scrambing to the top
tiers. Their motto is *Força,
Equilibri, Valor y Seny*
("Strength, Balance, Courage
and Mindfulness").

Although he had lived most of his life in Paris, Pablo Picasso began his career as an artist in Barcelona. Virtually all of the images he painted during the Blue Period, of friends, beggars, prostitutes and landscapes, were inspired by the city.

Barcelona's Museu Picasso has a good selection, such as *Blue Portrait of Jaume Sabartés*, *Motherhood* and *Roofs of Barcelona*.

Picasso was a child prodigy. His first word was *lápiz* ("pencil"), and by the age of 13, he was a more accomplished painter than his art-teacher father.

"

Others have seen
what is and asked
why. I have seen
what could be and
asked why not.

"

Pablo Picasso

The legendary chef Ferran Adrià i Acosta was raised in Barcelona.

He was the head chef of the iconic El Bulli restaurant in Roses on the Costa Brava, and was voted the best in the world for 10 seasons running.

The Filmoteca de Catalunya public film library is in the heart of the vibrant El Raval neighbourhood.

Opened in 1981, it screens subtitled art house films, new and old, at great prices.

Where to go for Cava

El Xampanyet: This small, popular bar offers authentic Catalan cava and cuisine in the city centre (Carrer de Montcada, 22).

Can Paixano: Close to the beach and Port Vell, this traditional bar offers an unbeatable ambience and prices. (Carrer de la Reina Cristina, 7).

La Vinya del Senyor: Enjoy the views of the neighbouring Santa Maria del Mar cathedral from this smart wine bar. (Plaza Santa Maria, 5).

According to legend, the Gran Teatre del Liceu is cursed. Built in 1847, the opera house has periodically suffered devastating fires, the last of which was in 1994 when it burnt down in just three hours.

The rebuilt opera house opened its doors again in 1999.

The Sant Antoni book market, dating back to 1936, is the largest of its kind in the world.

On Sundays, from 8.30 am to 2.30 pm, parents bring their children to the stalls outside the historic market building to buy comics, swap trading cards and develop a love of books.

66

In Barcelona, things seem so different. For example, I know that it's traditionally the least Spanish city, but you'd never know they had a monarchy, coming here as a tourist – as opposed to the UK, where the Queen is probably the best-known animal, vegetable and/or mineral when it comes to overseas visitors.

99

Julie Burchill

The Barcelona Moco museum – "mo" for modern art and "co" for contemporary – opened its doors in 2021.

Housed in a 16th-century palace on Montcada street, just metres from the Picasso Museum, it showcases works by active artists like Banksy and Kaws alongside art from established names such as Andy Warhol and Mark Rothko.

On 31 October, on the eve of All Saints' Day, it's traditional to eat roasted chestnuts, sweet potatoes and other seasonal fare.

In the 18th century, the poor bell-ringers, who had to work all through the cold night, would fortify themselves with these foods together with a glass of muscatel.

Take a wander around the Christmas markets in Barcelona and you're sure to spot the little figurine of the *caganer*, literally, "the shitter".

This bare-bottomed, pooping figurine is regarded as an essential feature of the traditional nativity scene, and each year new ones are produced of the year's celebrities, such as politicians or sports people.

Carmen Amaya was born in into a gypsy family in 1913, in Barcelona's Somorrostro shanty town next to the sea. She became one of the most outstanding *bailaoras* (female flamenco dancers) of the 20th century, and the first to perform footwork reserved for the best male dancers.

She sometimes danced in high-waisted trousers as a symbol of her strong character.

66

I was born by the sea.
My life and my art were
born of the sea. My name is
Carmen Amaya y Amaya. I am
Amaya twice over, as both my
father and mother were called
Amaya. All the Amayas in the
world are my cousins.

99

Carmen Amaya

In the late 1960s, Barcelona-born artist Joan Miró donated four works of art to the city, to welcome those arriving by air, land or sea.

Visitors arriving by plane are greeted by a colourful ceramic mural on the facade of Terminal Two. For those arriving by sea, Miró designed the mosaic on the Pla de l'Os, on La Rambla just outside La Boquería market.

The Parc de l'Escorxador –
now Parc Joan Miró – was chosen
to place Miró's 22-m (72-ft) tall
Dona i Ocell ("Woman and Bird")
statue to greet visitors arriving
by car.

The fourth gift was the Joan Miró
Foundation on Montjuïc, which
holds more than 10,000 pieces of
art, including some of Miró's most
remarkable works.

"

More important than a work of art itself is what it will sow. Art can die, a painting can disappear. What counts is the seed.

"

Joan Miró

Great pride goes into planning the *Festa Major*, a buzzing street festival held in August, in the Gràcia district.

Local residents spend months confecting the colourful decorations of the streets and squares for the week-long event, which invariably includes concerts, popular dances, exhibitions, *castellers* (human towers) and *correfocs* (fire-runs).

Catalan artist Joan Fontcuberta invited people to send a photograph in response to the question, "What does freedom mean to you?" Four thousand of them were integrated into his ceramic mural "The World Begins With Every Kiss". It was installed in Plaça d'Isidre Nonell to commemorate the 300th anniversary of La Diada, the Catalan surrender in the War of Spanish Succession.

"

The sound of a kiss isn't as loud as a cannon, but its echo lasts a great deal longer.

"

**Inscription next to Joan Fontcuberta's mural
"The World Begins With Every Kiss"**

Filmed in Barcelona

Todo Sobre Mi Madre
(All About My Mother), Pedro Almodóvar, 1999

En Construcción
(Under Construction), José Luís Guerín, 2001

Pa Negre
(Black Bread), Agustí Villaronga, 2010

Vicky Cristina Barcelona,
Woody Allen, 2008

Salvador (Puig Antich),
Manuel Huerga, 2006

The Passenger,
Michelangelo Antonioni, 1975

L'Auberge Espagnole
(The Spanish Apartment), Cédric Klapisch,
2002

Biutiful
Alejandro González Iñárritu, 2010

The unmissable Museu Nacional d'Art de Catalunya (MNAC) offers a fascinating artistic journey, from the world's best Romanesque collection of mural paintings to Gothic, Modern and 20th-century art.

The Montjuïc Magic Fountains are one of the greatest shows in town and a free one at that.

No-one is left unmoved by the dazzling display of water and lights to the sound of Freddie Mercury and Montserrat Caballé's "Barcelona".

Barcelona-born tenor José Carreras is one of the world's greatest opera stars.

He made his debut on the operatic stage at the age of 11.

Barcelona is home to
over 20 Michelin-starred
restaurants with world-class
chefs at their helm, such as
Lasarte's Martín Berasategui
(Carrer de Mallorca, 259).

23 June is the summer solstice
and the Feast of Sant Juan.
It's one of the liveliest and longest
nights of the year in Barcelona.

Also known as the *Nit del Foc*
("Night of Fire"), it is celebrated
with parties, bonfires and
fireworks – and if you're in town,
it's impossible to miss!

The summer is a popular time for a *sardinada*, where people gather outside to eat grilled sardines.

They are eaten with *pa amb tomàquet*, bread with tomato and olive oil.

Barcelona is a bilingual city (Spanish-Catalan) and the language of instruction at school is Catalan.

There's also a vibrant international community, meaning that you can hear as many as 300 languages spoken on its streets!

A smidgeon of Catalan

Yes *Sí*

No *No*

Hello *Hola*

Goodbye *Adéu*

Please *Si us plau*

Thank you *Gràcies*

Do you speak English? *Parla anglès?*

A bottle of cava please
Una ampolla de cava, si us plau

Bon appetit! *Bon profit!*

Can I have the bill please?
El compte, si us plau?

Ada Colau is the first female mayor of Barcelona, elected in 2015 as part of the citizen platform, Barcelona En Comú. She was one of the founding members of the Platform for People Affected by Mortgages, set up in Barcelona in 2009 in response to the increase in evictions caused by unpaid mortgage loans in the wake of the 2008 financial crisis.

Of Barcelona's 55 museums,
neither the magnificent Fundació
Joan Miró, nor the mighty Museu
Nacional d'Art de Catalunya
(MNAC), nor even the avant-
garde Museu d'Art Contemporani
de Barcelona (MACBA) are
as popular as the beloved FC
Barcelona Museum, which receives
over 1.5 million visitors a year.

Born in the Catalonian town of Figueres, Salvador Dalí was a frequent visitor to Barcelona.

In the 1970s, he would often dine at Via Veneto, the Michelin-star restaurant, where he is reported to have once ordered a soup infused with flowers from a cemetery.

The lesser-known Barcelona football club is RCD Espanyol.

Founded in 1900, it is just a year younger than FC Barcelona. It was one of the 10 Spanish clubs that founded La Liga – the highest level in the Spanish football league system – back in 1929.

One of the most striking Catalan traditions is the *correfoc* ("fire-run"), an outdoor performance associated with local festivities, especially La Mercè.

People dress up as devils and other monstrous creatures, light fireworks and burning sticks, and dance in a procession to the sound of rhythmic drums.

The science museum
CosmoCaixa recreates
an Amazonian rainforest
ecosystem with its
"Flooded Forest" exhibit.
Featuring animals such as
piranhas and crocodiles,
it surprises visitors with
periodic tropical rain.

66

You feel like half of
your life is a vacation
when you go to these
Barcelona music festivals
and have all day to sound
check or go to the pool.

99

Hamilton Leithauser

The arrival of the warm
weather signals the beginning
of Barcelona's music
festival season.

The biggest is Primavera Sound,
held right next to the sea at the
Parc del Fòrum. It showcases
a mix of musical bands from
indie and electronic to pop, jazz,
metal and rock.

Barcelona in Books

Barça: A People's Passion,
Jimmy Burns, 2000

The Shadow of the Wind,
Carlos Ruiz Zafón, 2001

Barcelona, Robert Hughes, 1992

Homage to Catalonia, George Orwell, 1938

Cathedral of the Sea,
Ildefonso Falcones, 2006

Homage to Barcelona, Colm Tóibín, 2002

Ghosts of Spain, Giles Tremlett, 2006

The Time of the Doves,
Mercè Rodoreda, 1962

66

Even the moon
was embarrassed
by the beauty of
Barcelona.

99

Andrew Barger

CHAPTER
FOUR

Green Lungs

Although a densely populated city, Barcelona has a surprising wealth of greenery and nature.

Besides its nine beaches, it is full of enchanting parks and gardens as well as the "green lung" of Montjuïc Park, and the woods and rolling hills of Collserola Natural Park only a short jaunt away.

Barcelona had its "back turned on the sea" and had no real beach to speak of before the sweeping renovation that took place for the 1992 Olympics.

Today, there are nine beaches along the 4.5-km (3-mile) coastline.

66

Watching the sun
set over the
Barcelona horizon,
one never grows old.

99

Anonymous

Parc del Guinardó, in the neighbourhood of Horta-Guinardó, has some great viewpoints reached via walking trails through the pine trees. The best views are from "Bunkers del Carmel", the old fortifications of Turó de la Rovira constructed during the civil war to protect Barcelona.

Locals head up here with a cold bottle of beer on summer evenings to watch the sun set over the city.

Barcelona's biggest green space, Collserola Park, has an area of 84.65 sq km (33 sq miles).

The largest metropolitan park in the world, it is 22 times bigger than New York's Central Park.

The city's parks, gardens and public spaces are dotted with ping-pong tables. Bring your own bats and balls!

Europe's third-oldest amusement park, Tibidabo, built in 1905, perches on the hill of the same name on the outskirts of Barcelona. It is visible from almost anywhere in the city.

Tucked away and mostly visited
by locals, Parc del Laberint d'Horta
is Barcelona's oldest garden,
a jewel of botanic architecture
constructed at the end of the
18th century.

With its maze of geometric
pathways, it came to fame when it
was used as a shooting location
for the award-winning film
Perfume, the Story of a Murderer.

Parc de Cervantes is a rose lover's dream come true, with over 10,000 rose bushes (and 2,000 different species) laid out in flower beds and surrounded by lush green lawns.

In early May, the garden hosts Barcelona's International New Rose Competition.

Outdoor Pools Uncovered

CEM Parc de la Ciutadella
For a rooftop dip

Club Natació Atlètic-Barceloneta
Right by the sea

Piscina Municipal de Montjuïc
Panoramic views

Parque de la Creueta del Coll
Pool and park in a former quarry

Can Dragó (Nou Barris)
Great for families

Zona de banys del Fòrum
Saltwater pool

Hotel Rey Fairmont Juan Carlos I
A luxurious splash

Piscines Bernat Picornell
Olympic-size recreation

Park Güell, designed by Gaudí, includes sinuous and colourful forms, columns that look like tree trunks, animal figures and geometric shapes.

Park Güell's architectonic elements are decorated with mosaics made from small ceramic pieces.

They are cemented together with a technique called *trencadís*, which means "chopped" in Catalan.

One of the most photographed features of Gaudí's Park Güell is its colourful mosaic salamander, known as *el drac* ("the dragon").

66

Anything created
by human beings is
already in the great
book of nature.

99

Antoni Gaudí

Some of Barcelona's best beaches lie just outside the city.

Half an hour away by bus, Ocata Beach is a hidden gem with fine golden sand and pristine water.

Near the Poblenou district and connected by a bike path, Mar Bella Beach is secluded, has a naturist section, and is popular with the LGBTQ crowd and the young.

For windsurfers, it's the place to catch some waves or, if you're a newbie, to take one of the courses offered by the Base Nàutica.

Every summer, the Montjuïc Castle gardens are transformed into a huge outdoor cinema showing classic and recent films.

Equipped with a picnic and blanket, people head up there to escape the city heat and to enjoy a fabulous viewing experience.

Barcelona's seafront promenade today features world-class sculpture on a grand scale, from Frank Gehry's giant golden fish to Rebecca Horn's *Wounded Shooting Star.*

The Parc de la Ciutadella was created for the 1888 Universal Exhibition and is one of Barcelona's major green hearts.

One of its best-known and most photographed monuments is Júlia, a life-size woolly mammoth statue that has stood amongst the trees and bushes for more than a hundred years.

Chilling in Parc de la Ciutadella

Row a boat on the lake

Feed the ducks

Visit the zoo

Admire the sculptures

Visit the epic Grand Cascade

Have a picnic

Take the kids to the playground

Play table tennis

If you fancy a bite with your feet in the sand and a sea view, but don't want to forgo quality, look no further than Xiringuito Escribà on the waterfront of Bogatell Beach. It serves up rice dishes, seasonal seafood and excellent appetizers – and be sure to save some room for one of its delicious cakes or desserts.

The Joan Brossa Gardens
is one of three leafy
Montjuïc parks named after
a Catalan poet.

Among the cedars, pines and
cypresses, it has some great
play spaces, such as sandpits,
musical paths, zip wires and
climbing structures.

CHAPTER
FIVE

These Streets Were Made for Walking...

The recent expansion of the cycle lanes makes Barcelona the ideal city for hopping on a bike – if you don't mind the odd hill.

Equally, the short distances within the city and its comprehensive, economical Metro and bus services make getting about easy. However, to get a real feel for the city? There's nothing like your own two feet...

66

Barcelona is a very old city in which you can feel the weight of history; it is haunted by history. You cannot walk around it without perceiving it.

99

Carlos Ruiz Zafón

Barcelona prides itself on having one of the most accessible public transport networks in Europe.

In fact, 147 metro stations out of 161 are completely accessible for people with reduced mobility and 100% of all city buses have motorized access ramps, wide doors and reserved seats.

Barcelona is well set up for night owls.

The Metro runs non-stop on a Saturday night and the NitBus (the night bus service) runs 17 different bus routes, 16 of which go through Plaça Catalunya at the heart of the city.

66

With her enchanting songs, her rare beauty, and clever tricks, this wild 'wanderess' ensnared my soul like a gipsy-thief and led me foolish and blind to where you find me now. The first time I saw her, fires were alight. It was a spicy night in Barcelona. The air was fragrant and free.

99

Roman Payne

Horse-drawn trams were introduced to the city in 1872, closely followed by steam trams in 1877.

Almost all the tramlines were phased out by 1971 to make room for the Barcelona Metro and buses. However, the start of the 21st century signalled the return of the tram with the opening of the Trambaix and Trambesòs networks.

In a city as compact as Barcelona, your own two feet are definitely the best – and cheapest – way to get about town.

This is supported by local government schemes aimed at widening pavements, and reducing the number of lanes on roads as well as the speed limits for traffic.

66

We crossed spacious streets,
with buildings resembling palaces,
in La Rambla promenade; the
shops were well illuminated and
there was movement and life…
I did not decide to go to sleep,
even though I wished to, so I could
rise early and contemplate, in
daylight, this city, unknown to me:
Barcelona, capital of Catalonia.

99

Hans Christian Andersen

To learn about the city from a different perspective, you can take a local tour through Barcelona's historic 19th-century sewers, the foundations of which were laid in medieval times.

Beneath the streets, you'll find a fascinating world. As water quietly flows, illuminated by dim fluorescent lights, the city's hustle and bustle continues on above.

66

There was much to be seen.
Where was I to begin, and where
to end, on the Rambla, the
Boulevard of Barcelona? ... The
Rambla became more and more
thronged; the excessively long
street became transformed into a
crowded festival-saloon.

99

Hans Christian Andersen, *In Spain* (1864)

Located in Barcelona's Ciutat Vella, the shopping street Portal de l'Àngel is the only Spanish street to feature on the ranking of the 25 most expensive commercial streets in the world.

It's also the country's busiest pedestrian street, with an average of 150,000 people walking down it every day.

Barcelona was the first and, to date, has been the only city to be awarded the prestigious Gold Medal for Architecture by the Royal Institute of British Architects. Many of its Catalan Art Nouveau treasures can be seen while strolling through the Eixample district.

Barcelona has 240 km (150 miles) of cycle lanes and one of the most successful public bike-sharing schemes in the world, Bicing.

You can take a boat ride on the Golondrinas (meaning "swallows") all the way from the Drassanes wharf across to the Olympic Marina and the Port Fòrum.

The first Golondrina cruises were steam-powered and took sail in 1888, on the occasion of Barcelona's first Universal Exhibition.

Smooth floors, all-year-round great weather, and superb architecture and street culture make Barcelona an ideal skater's playground.

Though the city has multiple open-air skate parks, the action centres on Plaça dels Àngels, opposite the Museum of Contemporary Art of Barcelona (MACBA) – known to locals as the "MACBA square".

CHAPTER
SIX

City of Secrets

The Catalan capital echoes with thousands
of memories from its past. Not just the big
sights, but every alleyway, square and corner
has a tale to tell of its long history and
unique culture.

Take a moment and look closely – the streets
will begin to reveal their secrets.

❝

By day the old area of
Barcelona is bustling, full of
shouting, hammering, drilling
and shutters being pulled up and
down. You listen out for sounds.
If you want a replacement gas
cylinder you wait for the sound of
the delivery man hitting a cylinder
with a piece of metal in the street.

❞

Colm Tóibín

The Mercat del Born was Barcelona's first market hall, and the largest of its kind in Europe.

After the city's central food market was relocated in 1971, it was abandoned until 2002, when work began to convert it into a library. However, the library project came to an abrupt halt when diggers came across important 17th- and 18th-century remains.

The archaeological site is now an exhibition centre named El Born Centre de Cultura i Memòria.

How to Order Coffee in Barcelona

Cafè sol (*café solo* in Spanish) –
If you only mutter "café", you'll get an
espresso, strong and bitter

Tallat (*cortado*) – An espresso with a splash
of steamed milk in a tiny cup

Cafè amb llet (*café con leche*) – A shot of
espresso and steamed milk, in equal parts

Cafè americà (*café americano*) –
An espresso diluted with hot water

Cafè amb gel (*café con hielo*) – A basic
café solo served alongside a glass of ice.

Voted best food market in the world by CNN, La Boqueria is a temple of gastronomy, with more than 300 stalls.

Visitors include some of the city's top chefs, who come to source the best produce and find inspiration for new recipes.

Perch on a stool at famed tapas bar El Quim de la Boqueria and try its fried eggs with baby squid, oxtail risotto, or foie gras with caramelized onion and wild mushroom.

Each year, on 23 April,
love is in the air as Catalonia
celebrates the patron saint
Sant Jordi, and millions of
books and roses are exchanged.

The main meeting point in
Barcelona is La Rambla, which
is packed from top to bottom
with book and flower stalls.

"

To travel across
Spain and finally to reach
Barcelona is like drinking
a respectable red wine and
finishing up with a bottle
of champagne.

"

James A. Michener

Legend has it that the Paris Eiffel Tower was pitched to Barcelona first, but the project was deemed to be too radical by Spain and did not fit the city's aesthetics!

If you see crowds turn up in town squares to dance in circles after church, that's the local dance, the *sardana*.

It's a fairly solemn affair and a vital symbol of Catalan cultural identity.

Carrer de la Princesa 11,
in the El Born district,
is home to El Rei de la
Màgia, one of the world's
oldest magic shops and
museums.

Patatas Bravas

One of Spain's most popular tapas, this simple dish consists of fried potatoes topped with a spicy sauce. Here are five of the best places to sample it in Barcelona.

El Tomás de Sarrià
(Major de Sarrià, 49)

Elsa y Fred
(Carrer del Rec Comtal, 11)

La Taverna del Clínic
(Carrer del Rosselló, 155)

La Esquinica
(Passeig de Fabra i Puig, 296)

Fàbrica Moritz
(Ronda de Sant Antoni, 41)

At the time of Barcelona's Corpus Christi celebrations, the courtyards of historic buildings in the Gothic Quarter are adorned with flowers and an egg "dances" on top of the fountain, suspended on the water jet.

It's a tradition dating back to medieval times, with the egg said to represent the body of Christ or the circle of life.

Flores Navarro is the florist that never sleeps.

Open 24 hours a day, 365 days a year, you can find it in the Mercat de la Concepció in the Eixample district (Carrer de València, 320).

While Barcelona is predominantly sunny, it actually has more annual rainfall than London!

The wettest month is October with an average of 87 mm (3.4 in) of rain.

The hottest months are July and August, with average day temperatures of around 82–84 °F (28–29 °C).

On Christmas Day every year, swimmers leap into the icy water in Port Vell and race 200 m (656 ft) across the harbour.

Launched more than a century ago, the event has only been suspended three times, during the civil war years.

Barcelona's most infamous men's prison was named the Model because it exemplified penitentiary reform at the turn of the 20th century. It contained rooms for exercise and reading, and even had a barber.

However, following the civil war, it became a place where political opponents were tortured and executed and a symbol of Francoist repression.

It closed its doors as a prison in 2017 and today is open to visitors.

The Plaça de Sant Jaume square, which today houses the Catalan government and the City Hall, has been the political centre of Barcelona since Roman times. There was a forum here, dominated by a temple dedicated to Emperor Augustus.

11 September commemorates the National Day of Catalonia (the *Diada*), marking the fall of Barcelona in the War of the Spanish Succession in 1714.

Since 2012, the Catalan independence movement has staged mass rallies in Barcelona on this day.

The Montjuïc Cemetery, built in the late 19th century, contains elaborate tombs in styles from Art Nouveau to Neo-classic and Gothic.

It has distinct sections for different groups of people – Catholics, Protestants, Jews, atheists, foreigners and gypsies all have their own separate areas.

Barcelona's Metro has an extensive network of 165 stations. But there are also 12 abandoned "ghost stations". If you keep your eyes open travelling on Line 2 or 5, you can catch a glimpse of the Gaudí station, built in 1968, but never opened.

Travellers claim to have seen mysterious ghost figures waiting for a train on the platform, and some even say they have seen Antoni Gaudí himself.

Casa Batlló, a Gaudí masterpiece, was intended by the architect to be a residential building.

Known as the "house of bones" or "house of the dragon", the balconies look like the bony jaws of a beast and the roof represents Sant Jordi (Saint George) and the dragon. It is built in the form of an animal's back, with shiny scales that change colour as you walk around.

More than 400 sculptures of dragons hide around the streets and buildings of Barcelona.

Legend tells that the first dragons arrived in Catalonia in the 15th century, along with the story of Sant Jordi and the slaying of the dragon.

You can find examples in Casa Amatller, the Palau de la Generalitat (the "Umbrella House") or Park Güell.

When it opened in 1848, Plaça Reial was one of the most distinguished squares in the city, and the only one with porticoes. However, by the 1960s it had fallen into disrepair and was known for begging, prostitution and drugs.

The square was given a fresh lease of life at the turn of the century, with elegant cafés, restaurants and nightclubs set up under the arcades.

While, strictly speaking, Barcelona has a population of 1.6 million within its city limits, there are over 3.2 million people in the metropolitan area, which includes neighbouring cities and towns.

Barcelona has earned a reputation as southern Europe's innovation hub.

The 22@ innovation district is now home to more than 1,500 companies in knowledge-intensive areas, information and computer technology (ICT), media, bio-medical, energy and design.

The Cathedral cloister, set back
from the busy streets of the Gothic
Quarter, encloses a charming
courtyard filled with tall palm trees
and a pond with a fountain.

It is home to 13 white geese
representing, according to tradition,
the age of Saint Eulalia, the
city's patron saint, when she was
martyred.

66

Allow me to state
here how much I love
Barcelona, an admirable
city, a city full of life,
intense, a port open to the
past and future.

99

Le Corbusier, architect